From the Small Business Primer Series

I0471065

Small Business Planning:
How to Plan—Without Writing a Business Plan

by

Bob Foster

Copyright Page

Copyright © 2013 by Bob Foster

ALL RIGHTS RESERVED. No part of this book may be reproduced or transmitted for resale or use by any party other than the individual purchaser who is the sole authorized user of this information. All other reproduction or transmission of any form, or by any means, electronic or mechanical, including photocopying, recording, or by any informational storage or retrieval system, is prohibited without express written permission from the author.

Contact:
bob@business-solutions-and-resources.com

Website:
www.business-solutions-and-resources.com

Cover design and graphics by Dhyana Kearly
www.dhyzen.com

Small Business Planning: How to Plan — Without Writing a Business Plan

Table of Contents

Books by Bob Foster

Be Your Own Turnaround Manager: A Common Sense Guide to Managing a Business Crisis

Business Survival Reality: The Mystery of Business Births and Deaths in the U.S.

Small Business Planning: How to Plan – Without Writing a Business Plan

Bootstrapping: And Other Alternative Ways to Finance Your Small Business

Small Business Financial Statements: What They Are, How to Understand Them, and How to Use Them

All books available at Amazon.com, and other booksellers.

"Vision without action is a daydream. Action without vision is a nightmare." —Japanese Proverb

Introduction

This book is one of my *Small Business Primer Series* books, and is directed primarily at the aspiring entrepreneur and the newer small business owner — those who have little experience with planning for their small business.

There is a mountain of information available from the Internet, and many other sources, on how to write a Business "Plan," but very little on how to "plan" the starting and running of your small business.

In truth, the frequently stated requirement that you must write a Business Plan is simply not true! You shouldn't believe everything you read about small business plans — neither their use, nor how they must be written.

This belief in business plans persists because most business gurus and pundits believe that the only startups worth discussing are high-technology ventures with the potential of becoming large, high-profit corporations.

The truth is: These "darlings" of the startup world comprise a *very* small portion of new business startups.

Of the over 6 Million new full-time businesses that start up each year (*Kauffman Index*), only about 1,000 will receive start up venture capital funding.

Consequently, I want to direct the information in this book to the large *majority* of the 6+ Million entrepreneurs who are starting up a new full-time business, and need to know how to properly "plan" for their new business.

Unfortunately, many new entrepreneurs do not believe they even need to do business planning. Many entrepreneurs believe it is a waste of time to try writing down their ideas and plans for starting and running their small business.

If you are one of the "I-don't-need-no-plans" types, be sure to read Chapter 1 in this book, titled *"Why Write Down* Any *Plans?"* The evidence is overwhelming that poorly planned businesses are doomed to failure.

As you will see, there is a big difference between "planning" and writing a "Business Plan," and this is discussed in Chapter 2.

Methods for recording your written "planning" are discussed in Chapter 3, along with the method that I think works best — *The Planning Workbook.*

However, there will be times when you do have to share your plans with other people, such as: bankers, suppliers, advisors, partners, investors, family, and friends. We'll discuss this situation in Chapter 4, *Sharing Your Plans.* This chapter covers what to share, and what not to share.

When sharing your business planning there are several different ways to do that depending on who will be reviewing the information. I have described the most important types of plan-sharing documents in: Chapter 5 – *Writing the Business Blueprint*; Chapter 6 – *Planning for Partnerships*; and Chapter 7 – *A Business Plan for Investors*.

If you will need professional investor financing for your business, there is one document that is extremely important — investors call this an *Executive Summary*.

Because of the importance of the Executive Summary, I have devoted an entire chapter to it — Chapter 8.

For the very few of you who will be seeking professional investor money (from Angel investors or Venture Capitalists), I have included a chapter on making a "Pitch" to an investor. More financing deals are lost at this point than ever get financed. Do it right or don't bother doing it at all. This is discussed in Chapter 9 – *The Pitch*.

In the last chapter (Chapter 10), I cover the issue of *Business Expansion Planning*, because this type of planning is quite different from planning a startup.

Although there are some chapters that discuss business "Plans," I want to emphasize that the majority of new startup businesses will never need to write a formal business "Plan" — but *will* need to maintain their written "planning."

That is everything you will find in this book, so, let's get started with a look at *"Why Write Down* **Any** *Plans?"* in the first chapter.

Chapter 1 —

Why Write Down *Any* Plans?

It's true that most businesses do not need to write a Business Plan, but that doesn't mean you do not need to do ongoing planning for your business — and record that planning in writing.

Too many entrepreneurs believe that *planning* takes too much time and energy. I often hear; "Why can't I just start my business and run it ... it's more difficult to write down 'plans' than it is to just-do-it."

Well, there are many reasons why you should write down your business planning. The information below has been circulating through the business world for quite some time — so consider the following well:

Some years ago, Yale University conducted a study that found 3% of Yale graduates had more wealth, years later, than the other 97% ***combined.***

Harvard Business School did a study on its' students 10 years after graduation and found that:

— 27% of them needed financial assistance.

— 60% of them were living from payday to payday.

— 10% of them were living comfortably.

— **Only 3% of them were financially independent.**

Why is there such a drastic difference between the top 3% and all the others? It doesn't stop with these university studies either. Let's look at some additional information:

From a more recent study sponsored by the *Ford Foundation*:

23% of the population has no idea what they want from life and as a result they have very little.

67% of the population has a general idea of what they want, but they don't have any plans for how to get it.

Only 10% of the population has specific well-defined goals, but even then, 7 out of 10 of these people reach their goals only half the time.

The top 3%, however, achieved their goals 89% of the time.

What is the significance of this 3% number that keeps popping up in various studies? Well, it is really quite simple ... in every case of the successful 3% (and only the 3%) — they *wrote down their goals.*

Dreams and wishes are not goals until they are written on paper as specific desired results. In some real sense, writing them down materializes them and brings them to life.

The experts claim that the act of writing makes an imprint on the brain that helps set the direction of actions by a person.

If that does not address your question of *Why Write Down Any Plans?* Then here is ....

More Reason Yet

Still not convinced why you should write down your business plans? How about this: A recent report from the *Office of Advocacy of the U.S. Small Business Administration* cited the *Panel Study of Entrepreneurial Dynamics*, which stated, "Entrepreneurs who completed their business planning were six times more likely to start a business [than those who did not]."

And, "Those who completed written planning were likely to engage in more startup activities than those whose plans were unwritten ..."

These are pretty compelling reasons as to why you should write down your business planning. And of course, if you are going to seek outside financing from family and friends, a bank, Angel Investor, or Venture Capitalist, they will all expect you to have written plans.

I also know from experience that as you are about to move from your pre-venture planning to actual startup planning you can hit the wall of information overload and begin to wonder if you can really pull this off — doubts start to creep in.

That's when you spend a good deal of time reviewing your business planning to reassure yourself that you have covered every base you know of at this time. You may do this countless times before you see your first dollar of revenue.

So, now that we are convinced we need to write down our business planning, let's take a look at how best to do that.

We can start with a discussion, in the next chapter, on what it means to "plan" vs. writing a *Business Plan*.

Chapter 2 —

Planning vs. A Plan

There are two separate aspects of business planning, (1) building a Business Model, and (2) writing a Business Plan.

The Business Model

If you read the prior chapter, you will understand that if you want to have a successful business you really need to write down not just your business plans, but your life plans as well.

This becomes the "model" for every aspect of your business — and life. Whether you realize it at this point or not, your business will become the biggest part of your life for as long as you own the business. So, plan well!

How and where you do this is not really important — nothing needs to be formal … it can just be a few scribbles on cocktail napkins, a loose-leaf file full of your thoughts and ideas, a 3-ring binder, or a wall covered with butcher paper … whatever helps you record your visualization and thinking.

The Business Plan

Unless you need to solicit professional investors for money to finance your business, you will likely never need to write a Business Plan describing how you are going to run your new business, and how you are going to make an investor a lot of money.

A Business Plan is not really a "model" of your business, because it is static, not dynamic. It is more a record of what, who, why, when, and the expected results from your business — *as you visualized them at the moment you created the document.*

So.....

Why Separate the Two?

How many times have you been told, or read somewhere, that it is essential for you to create a complete "Business Plan" in order for your business to succeed?

Well relax, because for the vast majority of new, existing, and getting-ready-to-start businesses out there — this is a myth.

Not only is it a myth — creating a "Business Plan" can actually be harmful to many businesses.

Yes, you have to write things down, as we just read in the previous chapter, but you can do it your way ... you don't have to follow some special format prescribed by people who have never started a business like yours.

The only exception to this myth busting is if you are going to make a formal request for money from a Venture Capitalist, or some of the Angel Investors. Just bear in mind that less than one-tenth of one percent of all new startups this year will receive investor money from these two sources.

The great majority of what is being talked about today regarding business plans is directed at the high-tech/Internet/high-profit-potential businesses that are looking for substantial outside investment.

These are the "darlings" of the startup world and receive most of the attention from the media, pundits, and business gurus. Everyone is looking for the next *Google* or *Facebook*.

You might even be surprised to learn that many people consider these high-tech businesses to be the *only* new businesses that should be called a "startup."

Just remember that of the 6+ Million new startups each year, only about 1,000 of these startup "stars" will receive start up money from Venture Capitalists.

However, in the event your new startup is actually in this small group of businesses that might attract venture capital, I have included a chapter later in this book devoted to writing the formal investor-directed "Business Plan."

But first—consider this:

"Plans are useless, but planning is essential." --Dwight D. Eisenhower (*From a speech to the National Defense Executive Reserve Conference in Washington, D.C. – November 14, 1957*)

I've also heard it stated "Plans are only good until they come in contact with your first customer." In other words, when a Business Plan begins to get implemented, the static nature of a formal document just will not be able to keep up with the reality of the business world.

Formal, printed Business Plans cannot be modified, updated, and reprinted fast enough to keep up with your ideas, and the changes that will be coming in your business—but changes *can* be quickly updated in your own personal planning format.

These quick response changes can often mean the difference between success and failure for your small business.

So, we have "planning" as the foundation for building your business, and the "Business Plan" as the means for communicating your plans (of the moment) to investors.

Let's be sure we keep these two distinctions clearly separated in our minds as we proceed through this book.

Just in case I have confused you, the point is ... you *do* need to plan, and plan carefully, but you *do NOT* need to follow the prescribed formats of a "Business Plan" that are usually laid down by the business gurus of the day.

Remember, your planning is not for professional investors — it is for you, and you can write down whatever you want.

And, as we have already discussed, you do *need* to write down, somewhere, all your thoughts, ideas, visions, and calculations ... and then use them as the basis for ongoing planning as you build your business model.

I will cover how I think is the best way to record your planning, in the next chapter "*The Planning Workbook.*"

Chapter 3 —

The Planning Workbook

To me, this is the key chapter in this book. How well you perform the steps outlined in this chapter may largely determine how well your business will succeed.

As I said in the previous chapter, you do not need any kind of "formal" document to try and follow while you are running your business.

But, I think we have also established that it is essential to write down everything we are planning, for, and about, our business ... and our life.

In addition, every time something changes, or needs to be changed, that is also written down. (Be advised — plans change.)

In summary, this form of business planning is basically a written record of your thoughts, ideas, research, calculations, estimates, etc. for your business — and your life, during the time you own and run your business.

So, whether you write it all down on cocktail napkins, a Whiteboard, or a school tablet, it really doesn't matter. Just be sure to write down everything ... to imprint it on your brain.

19

Personally, I like to use a 3-ring binder with sheet dividers set up for major planning categories. This method allows me to look at whatever category I want to research, or update, at the moment without doing a lot of hunting around.

It still shouldn't be a "formal" document however. I may use a combination of handwritten pages and notes, Word.doc pages, and Excel spreadsheets. Regardless of the format or material that is in this binder, I can jot notes or change whole sections very easily.

I call this binder my *Planning Workbook*, and it gradually becomes a manual for my "business model," and the roadmap for how that business is going to get to its' intended destination.

Jane — The Entrepreneur

In other books in my *Primer Series* I created a fictitious person, named "Jane — The Entrepreneur," as an example of how she planned, financed, and started her business. So here, let's take a look at Jane's planning process.

Jane had just gone through some difficult times in her life, and she now needed to take control of her situation and her life. She had to define and write down where she wanted her life to go — what her goals in life were. And she had to write down her plans on how to get there.

So, let's take a look at what might have been Jane's *Planning Workbook* as she began to plan for changes in her life, and how she was going to realize those changes.

Jane set up 14 separate sections in her 3-ring binder. Each of these sections are described in the following:

Section 1 — Life Plan

This is the section where Jane outlined her situation. She had been downsized, unemployed, homeless, and living with her sister. She needed to set some new goals for her life. This is where she wrote down where she was today, and what her new goals for her life were.

This section would also be where Jane wrote down in some detail why she wanted to start a business, instead of just being an employee somewhere.

Jane also wrote down the type of business she would like to start. She would include details here that were only meaningful to her.

This is where Jane could let her imagination run free — she wrote in graphic detail just what she wanted in her business.

And, of course, she could add, or change, any of her goals or thoughts anytime she thought about something new.

There are a couple of important things to keep in mind when creating this section of the workbook:

(1) – Goals must be clear and concise with lots of action verbs. There must be start dates and milestone dates.

(2) – Goals must not be confused with "tasks." There are other sections in your Planning Workbook where you will record and track your "tasks." Consider building a house ... having the house would be the goal – how you build the house would be a matter of tasks, and schedules.

Section 2 - Entrepreneurship

This is where Jane faced the elephant in the room—could she really become an entrepreneur? This question takes a lot of soul-searching, because starting a business is actually starting a new life, and not everyone is equipped to do that.

Everyone who thinks about starting a business should face up to this issue and look deep into themselves before making an offhand assumption that entrepreneurship is not that difficult.

I have written extensively about what it takes to be an entrepreneur, and you can access this free information at: http://www.business-solutions-and-resources.com/what-is-an-entrepreneur.html This is an important issue, so don't gloss over it.

Here is where Jane described her lack of business knowledge, and then set training goals for learning how to start and run a successful business. She could also begin working on these goals immediately by attending local workshops, reading, specific adult education classes, etc.

Note: *No one but you will ever see your Planning Workbook, so don't be afraid to delve into your personal feelings and desires, and write them down here ... it's very important that you do.*

Section 3 - Business Description

This is the section where Jane visualized her business through the eyes of customers. Here, she laid out in detail how she wanted her business to run, and what she wanted the customer experience to be.

Jane wanted the culture of her business to be fun, enjoyable for employees, and uplifting to customers. Not over-the-top crazy, but a fun place to work, visit — and make money.

If you read about Jane in the *"Bootstrapping"* book in my *Primer Series*, you know that she wanted to open a neighborhood coffee shop, and she wanted the customer experience to be second to none in her community.

Don't be conservative at this point — let your imagination run free and write down all that you would like to see happen with your new business — even if it seems pretty ridiculous at this point.

Jane's intended product and business was commonplace — only her approach to how she described her business was tailored to her. But, if your intended business revolves around a unique product or service, you could outline that here in this section, or create an entire new section to do that.

As you get further along in your planning you can always come back to this section and summarize a more precise description of what your business will look like in its various stages of growth.

This section is a "work in progress" for the entire life of your business; so don't be shy about writing down your vision.

Section 4 - Market

This section is the first place where Jane began to apply the knowledge she was getting from her new business training. She knew there had to be a market opportunity for the business she just described in her workbook, or else all her visions would become … just dreams.

In Jane's planning, she wanted a brick and mortar store, so she had to have walk-in customers — she needed a location that would provide that.

Jane knew she had to have a product that people would buy, and a location that made it convenient for them.

This is where most business planning runs off the track, because new entrepreneurs too often let their passions cloud there thinking. To have a successful startup you need to learn about your potential market, and in order to learn — you need to "leave the building."

So Jane picked out a few likely locations for her business, and physically spent time at these locations looking for the following:

— *Was there heavy pedestrian traffic of people on their way to work? She counted street and sidewalk traffic.*

— *How old were they?*

— *How many people were carrying cups of coffee?*

— *What were the names on the coffee cups (where did the coffee come from)?*

— *Were they blue-collar, or white-collar workers?*

— *How close would her competition be?*

— *Did her competition have drive-thru windows?*

— *How many cars used the drive-thru? (Jane counted them.)*

— *How long did they have to wait for their coffee?*

— *Was her potential market large enough to support her business.*

— *Did the demographics match her selected locations.*

— *And many other things that Jane observed while onsite.*

Jane wrote down all her observations and findings in her Planning Workbook, and then spent time analyzing her data.

Note: *This is where it gets tough, because if your market analysis indicates there might not be a large enough market at those sites — or at all — it would be time to move on to a new location, or a new business idea.*

However, from this analysis Jane determined not only that her business idea was viable, but she also knew what the best area would be for her neighborhood coffee shop — and she had the data to prove it.

In addition, this research and analysis gave Jane a good understanding of what kinds of advertising and PR programs would best reach her intended customers.

Section 5 - Employees

Many home-based businesses will not need employees, but most of them will use independent contractors at some point in their growth. So, this section of the workbook could be used to record information on outsourcing work instead of details about hiring employees.

In Jane's case, she would need to hire employees, so she wrote down the traits she would be looking for in her employees. She also needed to think about where she would find these "perfect" employees for her business.

Just as important as describing her desired employee, Jane needed to set out her objectives for how to make the jobs she would be offering truly meaningful to her employees. Study after study points out that job satisfaction — through meaningful work — is more important than wages or benefits.

This is a tough issue and takes a great deal of thought and creativity. Jane wrote down everything that came to mind, and then formed a vision of what it would be like to work in her coffee shop.

This visualization is the force behind what will create and maintain a business's culture.

Also, be sure to constantly update this section of your workbook with your successes and failures—what worked and what didn't. This will fine tune your hiring skills and further refine your business's culture.

Section 6 - Facilities

This is usually a minor concern for home-based businesses, but still needs to be addressed. Most home businesses need a comfortable place to work that serves as an enticement to want to work there.

Certain home-based service businesses (plumbers, electricians, contractors, etc.) need a place to make calls, update their financial records, invoice customers, plan out their advertising and PR programs, work on their Planning Workbook, etc. Some of them may also need a place to store some of their tools or inventory.

Put all your desires and needs down in this section of your workbook.

In Jane's case, she wanted a storefront shop in her desired location—brick and mortar real estate. In addition, she sketched out her desired layout of the shop (with several alternatives).

She talked to Realtors and Property Managers about space availability and costs. She needed to determine what she could expect in Landlord improvements for her business, and what improvements she would need to finance herself.

This was an educational process for Jane, so she wrote down everything she learned about obtaining her desired facility.

So, whatever you think your needs will be, write them all down in this section of your workbook and update it as often as you come up with a thought, or new information.

Section 7 - Equipment

When Jane had the previous sections of her Planning Workbook pretty well under way, it was time for her to start thinking about what equipment she would need for her business.

Many new businesses will not need much in the way of equipment, but others, like Jane's business, will need substantial equipment to operate their business.

Jane started by making a list of all the items she thought she would need and then put estimated costs beside them. She kept adding to this list, and updating the costs as she obtained more information, or determined some additional item of equipment she would need.

A word of caution here — do not include any items that are just "nice-to-have" things. For a small startup like Jane's you want to think in terms of "essential" items only. Maybe you can add some of the others as you grow — but not as a startup.

Depending on your business, you may want to earmark those items that you absolutely must have to start your business vs. those you will subsequently need later to expand and grow your business.

The objective here is usually to minimize, as much as possible, the amount of start up money you will need.

Also, in order to keep costs down don't turn your back on used or refurbished equipment.

This could be the first place a spreadsheet might be used. It could be handwritten on multi-column paper, or you could construct it on your computer if you prefer.

Set up column 1 for a description of the item; column 2 for the estimated cost; column 3 for the quantity required; column 4 for the total cost for each item description; column 5 for preferred vendor; and column 6 for any notes you care to make.

Then of course, you would have a grand total at the bottom of column 4 — the total cost of all equipment you think you will need to start your business.

This spreadsheet can be easily updated every time new information is obtained. If your spreadsheet is on your computer, I suggest periodically printing a copy of it and putting it in your 3-ring workbook binder — and make notes all over it.

Section 8 - Operations

Something that many new entrepreneurs don't take into proper consideration is the basic cost of running a business.

In the fictitious story of *Jane – the Entrepreneur*, she spent a good deal of time researching the requirements for permits, licenses, insurance, and setting up the proper business form. Jane wrote down everything she learned about government regulations and requirements.

These are things that are usually necessary for any type of business and should be investigated early in your research and written down in this section of your workbook.

This makes all the information readily available when you quickly need it.

Plus you will want to include the cost for all these items in your business's financial model when you build it later.

Section 9 - Inventory

In Jane's case, of course, she needed a certain amount of inventory before she opened her doors to her first customer. Jane would maintain an inventory of all food products she would need, plus disposables like napkins, plastic utensils, stirring sticks, paper coffee cups, etc.

This is also where a spreadsheet can come in handy. The initial layout could be exactly the same as the one described above for equipment, and then after the business starts up, an additional column or two could be used to track on-hand amounts and what has been ordered.

There is no need for any kind of automated inventory control system for most small businesses—just tracking the inventory numbers by hand on a simple spreadsheet is fast enough and adequate (don't spend money where it is not essential).

The original spreadsheet could be kept in your Planning Workbook and periodically updated with new, or changed items, and most recent costs. Later, this spreadsheet could be printed and used to record on-hand and on-order status.

Although maintaining your spreadsheets on a P.C., or other electronic devise, would make the job simpler and faster, don't let not having one stop you. This is not complicated and can be done manually just fine.

Section 10 - The Business's Financial Model

This is where Jane took all the "operating" costs she had identified in her Planning Workbook so far, and began to actually build a rough financial model of her new business. It's easier than you might think.

Jane started by constructing another spreadsheet, somewhat similar to the ones already discussed, except this spreadsheet would use column 1 to describe all the categories of income (Sales) or expense, and then an additional column where she would write her estimates for each of the next 12 months. A last column would be for the totals for each category.

We won't call this a Pro forma financial statement, since it is much too crude at this point — it is just Jane's best guess as to what her income and expenses *might* be over the first 12 months.

This look at her "operating" expenses would give her some indication of how many sales, or how much additional operating capital, she would need before she became profitable.

Also, note that nothing would have been committed to yet, and everything Jane had written about her business could be easily changed at this point.

It is important here to list every single thing that could possibly become an expense during the first year of starting up your business.

Jane had a good start, because she would have already researched and recorded costs for all the major operating expenses in prior sections of her workbook.

It was then just a matter of listing all these items on her spreadsheet and then adding a few descriptions like Utilities, Office Supplies, Contributions, Travel & Entertainment, etc.

For the moment, the costs for Leasehold Improvements, Equipment, and initial Inventory would not even be considered on this spreadsheet.

Section 11 - Advisory Board

By now, Jane was getting worried — she had pretty well exhausted all she had learned so far about starting a business. So she sought out her friendly banker who told her about forming an "Advisory Board."

An Advisory Board is simply a small group of experienced, local, business people who are willing to advise new, less experienced, aspiring entrepreneurs in their community. These people often serve with no, or minimal, compensation to help a small business get started.

So, Jane began her research on people in her community who might be good candidates for her advisory group. She made notes in her workbook on each person she thought might qualify.

She talked to her banker, Real Estate broker, insurance agent, the CEO of a local company, and several others to get information on various people who had previously served in an advisory capacity in the community. Every thing she learned about all these people she wrote down in her Planning Workbook.

Then, from the information in her workbook, she selected three names she thought would be the best fit for her and her upcoming business. When she approached them with her business story and request — they all accepted.

Jane then had a group of advisors who were successful in their own business endeavors ... and knew a lot more about starting a business than she did.

Section 12 - Accounting/Bookkeeping

One of the first things Jane's Advisory Board recommended was that she work with an Accountant to create a *Pro forma Statement of Financial Results*. This document is usually referred to as a *Pro forma P&L*. (Jane may have even had an Accountant on her Advisory Board.)

This is basically a spreadsheet combining all of the estimates of sales and costs she had previously written down in her Planning Workbook, plus those things that Jane had left out.

In addition, her Accountant would prepare a new spreadsheet showing all the cash requirements and where the cash might come from.

Jane then presented her set of *Pro forma Statements* to her Advisory Board, and they reviewed and commented on each line item on the pro forma.

Jane took many notes and then went back to the various sections of her workbook and reworked her assumptions and estimates based on the advice she was given by her Advisory Board.

Another meeting with her Accountant and Advisory Board, and Jane's Planning Workbook had a complete financial Business Model for her upcoming new business.

This financial business model would serve two purposes:

(1) - It was a dynamic model where she could establish budgets, and record actual performance against those budgets for each line item on the model. This would become a very integral part of her ongoing business model that she kept updated in her Planning Workbook.

By diligently updating her financial model Jane not only could analyze any differences between her budget and actual figures, but it would allow her to refine her budget numbers for future planning.

(2) - If Jane were going to need outside financing for her new business, her financial business model would be a key element in helping her prepare a separate planning document for outsiders.

In addition, the Accountant helped Jane set up a beginning set of accounting records, or "books," and directed her to a bookkeeping service that could keep her records up to date at little cost.

Her bookkeeping service, or Accountant, could then provide Jane with up to date and accurate financial statements.

If you have more interest in small business financial statements, you can refer to another book in the *Primer Series*, "*Small Business Financial Statements: What They Are, How to Understand Them, and How to Use Them.*" (Available at Amazon.com, and other book outlets.)

Whether you are going to need outside financing, or use your own money, a financial model is something you should include in the pre-venture preparation of your business.

Be prepared, as this is the place where reality usually hits hard, because your Advisory Board and your accountant will point out the details that you will have missed yourself.

It is very important to have a realistic business financial model in hand, along with your cash flow requirements at this point in your business planning.

Section 13 - Financing

Now things begin to get more serious — this is the point beyond which there is no return. Up until now Jane could have dropped the whole idea of starting a business, and there would have been no financial losses, or commitments to undo. Jane was only building a "Business Model" in her Planning Workbook.

So, Jane started by researching and investigating everything she could on how she might finance her new model business. Everything that Jane learned about financing, she wrote down in the Financing section of her Planning Workbook.

This is also what you will need to do as well — unless you already have adequate money on hand to start your business.

Statistically, the majority of new entrepreneurs will need to find sources of start up capital from somewhere, and I have written an entire book on the subject, titled *Bootstrapping: And Other Alternative Ways to Finance Your Small Business.* You can get more information about this book at http://bit.ly/10GBNT9 Or, you can order it direct from Amazon at http://amzn.to/Y2BBK2

In searching for money to start your business, you will need to share some of the information in your Planning Workbook. What and how much you share depends on where you are trying to raise capital.

The next chapter of this book discusses when you might need to share your planning information. Subsequent chapters then discuss how to present certain parts of your planning to prospective sources of start up money.

Section 14 - Startup

After Jane determined how she was going to finance her business, it was time to start planning the details of implementing all the plans she had completed so far.

This was also the most exciting time for Jane as this last section in her Planning Workbook is the culmination of everything she had planned for in all the previous sections.

A startup "checklist" usually becomes mandatory when creating this section. There are a myriad of things that need to be done before the doors open, or the first customer is faced. Keeping track of the status of them all is critical.

Jane referred to the section of her workbook where she had all the real estate information on obtaining her storefront and wrote down on her checklist all the things she had to do to complete that large task.

She did the same thing for her Equipment section, and her Inventory section, and so on. Without a detailed checklist, getting a business started can become overwhelming.

Of course she also constantly referred to her Planning Workbook to make sure she was planning her implementation around her milestone goals.

One thing Jane did, which most new entrepreneurs don't do, is make notes in her Startup section on what she did wrong, or didn't do that she should have, and what she did right, so when she started her next business she would have a head start on the actual startup process.

If you maintain your workbook in a timely fashion, you will easily determine the initial mistakes you made in your earlier planning—and therefore won't make again.

Perhaps more important, your workbook can serve as a repository for the many, many ideas you will constantly come up with over time.

Your Planning Workbook can then be used in planning how you're going to implement all those new ideas.

Time Required for Planning

It probably seems like Jane spent an awful lot of time doing all this planning and preparation. In this example, I created the worst possible scenario, in that Jane had no business training or experience when she started—and she had very ambitious business plans.

However, to gain the knowledge she needed, Jane could use the Internet, attend local business workshops, attend adult education classes, read books, find a mentor, and on and on. When you have entrepreneurial passion—you will find a way to gain the knowledge you need to make your dreams come true.

Yes, you may need to stop hanging out with friends, or going to clubs. You may have to substantially cut back on your social media time, or you may need to give up playing video games and watching TV—it all depends on how bad you want to have a successful business.

Over 5 million businesses will fail this year, and you can be sure that most of them did not do the pre-startup planning that Jane did. In most cases I would bet that they did very little "planning" at all. Remember: *Plans are useless, but planning is essential.*

A recent survey by *LegalZoom* indicated that 60% of entrepreneurs spent more than 6 months planning their business, and 21% spent one to three years in the planning stage. Only 9% spent less than a month planning before starting their business.

Of course, in Jane's situation she worked at her planning and training full time, but, because of the complexity of Jane's desired business, I could see her taking several months from the day she wrote down her goals to the day she started to implement the first item on her implementation checklist.

Obviously, this would depend on how quickly financing

could be obtained.

However, if you only have a few hours per day available, it could take you longer, unless you have a great deal of business knowledge or have started a business before.

One caveat: Don't spend so much time "planning" that you never get around to starting your business. Plan well—then do!

So, keep updating your business planning, even if it is just adding more cocktail napkins, or more sheets of butcher paper to the wall—although I think you will find something like the *Planning Workbook* makes the job a little easier and more complete.

If you do everything that Jane did with her workbook, you will have in your hands a complete business model that contains everything you need to actually start your business.

In addition, this model will serve you well throughout the entire growth of your business—as long as you don't neglect to keep it updated with your results, and your ideas.

As you get further into starting and running your business, you will discover that there are many people who will want to see your "Business Plan." Obviously, you are *not* going to show anyone your Planning Workbook, so you will need to provide some sort of condensed version of your business planning.

We're going to discuss what information you might want to share and how best to share it in the next chapter titled *"Sharing Your Plans."*

Chapter 4—

Sharing Your Plans

After you start to pull all your planning information together and are taking the first steps to starting your business, outsiders will begin to ask to see your "Business Plan."

Who might these people be? Let's take a look:

— The first people who will look at your planning will be members of your Advisory Board. These folks will need to see exactly what it is that you are planning for your business.

— Some city agencies may want to see what you intend to create with your new business idea before they issue any permits (but usually there are only forms to fill out).

— Your accountant will want to see some details of the research you did and the estimates you arrived at.

— A Realtor, or property management company may want to see a "Business Plan" (their term) before they lease any commercial property to you.

— If you ever need to borrow money from a bank, your banker will usually want to see your Business Plan.

— Suppliers of large equipment who finance equipment purchases or leases will likely want to see your plans to assure themselves that your business will be able to pay them.

— If you need a capital investment, or loan, from family and friends you will need to provide them with a simple document that explains your business and how you expect that business to perform.

— If you need a larger capital investment from Angel Investors or alternative funding, you will need to provide at least basic information about your business plans — although more and more alternative and Angel investing is done through their own formats for presenting information.

— If you are a high-tech startup looking for Venture Capital, you will need some sort of "official" Business Plan to present to Venture Capitalists.

You may run into other special situations where someone wants to see your Business Plan, but the above list probably includes most of the possibilities.

Actually, if you are going to self-finance your new business, you may not ever be required to give your planning information to anyone other than your Advisory Board.

So, what kind of document are you going to give these people when they ask? They really don't need to see a formal

50-page document (even the VCs), and obviously you are *not* going to give them a copy of your Planning Workbook.

Well, for just about everyone on the above list, I recommend a short 2 to 4-page compilation (plus the Appendix) of your business planning to date. This type of summary compilation should satisfy every need except for most (not all) professional investors.

I call this simple compilation a "Business Blueprint," and discuss how to write it in the next chapter, titled *Writing the Business Blueprint.*

There is also one area of business planning that is rarely addressed, and that is where there is more than one founder of the business, and the planning for that business is conducted by multiple parties — regardless of the way the business might be formally organized.

Since this is a fairly common situation, I have included a special chapter to discuss how to handle planning when there are partners involved. This is discussed in chapter 6, titled *Planning for Partnerships.*

Of course, there are always a few startups that are of the high-tech variety, and they seem to migrate heavily toward venture capital to fund their new business. As a result, I have included a chapter just for planning requirements for professional investors—both Angel Investors and Venture Capitalists. This is chapter 7, titled *Business Plan for Investors*.

There is one other type of Business Plan you may one day want to write—a business plan seeking money to make a substantial expansion of your growing business. I discuss this type of plan in chapter 9, titled *Business Expansion Plan*.

Recap

I hope I haven't scared anyone off with all this talk about writing a "Business Blueprint." I think you will see in the next chapter that for those few businesses that will ever need one, it is really very simple.

In the meantime, let's consider what we have discussed about small business planning in this book so far:

— Every business needs to plan

— Every business needs to write down their plans

— Every business needs to maintain constant planning

— Most businesses do not need to write a formal "Business Plan"

— Those businesses that might need to provide planning information to others can compile a simple "Blueprint" of their plans.

— Partnerships need to write a special plan for their business

— A very few businesses will need to write a complete "formal" Business Plan for investors.

Let's look at a simple compilation of your planning in the next chapter, titled *Writing the Business Blueprint.*

Chapter 5 —

Writing the Business Blueprint

We're calling this a "Business Blueprint," because it is in no way shape or form anything like the formal *Business Plan* depicted in most books and websites.

The assumption here is that the people you will be showing it to are not "professional" investors — they are family and friends and outside business related interests.

There is no strict format to this document and every time you prepare a copy you will need to visualize the person you are giving your Blueprint to.

As an example — let's say you are hoping to convince your Uncle Al to invest in your new business.

How close are you to this uncle? Does he know much about your business? Is he a favorite relative? Does he already invest in other businesses?

How many Business Plans has he previously read and analyzed? In other words, how experienced an investor is Uncle Al?

Now with these considerations in mind, you need to prepare your Business Blueprint tailored specifically for Uncle Al.

You can use information from various sections in your Planning Workbook, but at a minimum you should write your document to include the following information for this potential family investor:

— *A brief description of your new business ... depending on how much your audience (Uncle Al) already knows about your business. This also applies to any other relative or person you plan on talking to.*

— *A brief synopsis of your market, including who will buy what you're offering — and why. You should also cover how you intend to reach your target market, along with expected results.*

— *If you have a partner(s), or some key employee on board, or just waiting to join your new business, give a brief resume of these folks because your audience (Uncle Al) may not be familiar with them.*

— *You should briefly describe your Advisory Board — especially if there is a prominent local businessperson on the Board.*

— *You need to explain how far along you are on implementing your business plan ... especially if you are still in the pre-venture stage.*

— *Include summary financial numbers from your accountant's Pro forma P&L, and Cash Flow Statement, showing how much* money you are going to need, how much profit you plan to make, and how you intend to make Uncle Al's investment pay off.

— You should identify obstacles to making your business succeed, and how you intend to overcome them. This will head off many of the questions that Uncle Al might ask, and it will also give Uncle Al some confidence in your capability as an entrepreneur.

— If you have already started your business, you need to show how much you have spent to date, and for what, plus any income you might have received.

— Most important, you need to include in your Business Blueprint exactly what you are looking for in the way of investments or loans, and what you are willing to give up in stock, interest, etc. Typically, when dealing with family and friends, we are hesitant about asking for specific amounts, but this is business and you must be clear and concise about your business needs.

— Any supporting documents need to go in the Appendix. This could include copies of:

~Resumes of partners and/or key employees (if any).

~Actual financial reports (if any).

~Collateral material — brochures, advertising copy, etc. (if any).

~Any other supporting documents you feel are appropriate.

This *Business Blueprint* should not be very long — 2 to 4 pages at most, plus the Appendix. You don't need to write down everything — only "enough."

You only need to staple the pages together and you have your *Business Blueprint* for your Uncle Al — and a basic format for almost anyone who might ask for a copy of your "Business Plan," including other investors.

However, there is one special form of small business planning that seems to go largely unmentioned — planning for a business partnership. Let's look at this very important type of planning in the next chapter.

Chapter 6—

Planning for a Partnership

Let's assume that you and a close friend are starting a small business together.

You and your friend can hammer out business ideas on a white board, or your lunch napkins, as long as you both are working toward the same business goal.

Of course, you will want your attorney to prepare the proper partnership or corporate legal documents so that your business obtains a legal basis.

I strongly recommend that you do NOT try to prepare legal documents yourselves without at least having a legal overseer. I have seen the trauma caused down the road by improperly prepared initial legal documents.

A simple partnership agreement, or LLC, does not cost that much to have an attorney involved, and it is worth it in the long run.

A More Important Document

However, when creating a partnership, a very important issue needs to be addressed right at the start.

You and your friend need to develop a document outlining which of you will be responsible for what functions of the business. You can call this document anything you want, but for ease of use in this discussion, let's call it a "Duty Roster."

This is not a legal document—nor job descriptions—just a simple list outlining the division of work, and it could be written on scrap paper if you wanted, but preferably it should be a part of your Planning Workbook.

If there are more partners than just the two of you, everyone who is part of the startup needs to participate in the development of this document. They then need to sign it, in order to indicate they were a part of the planning discussions, and that they agree with the contents of the document.

Be aware that this Duty Roster is not to take the place of the planning discussed in prior chapters. The *Planning Workbook* should still serve as the manual on the Business Model you and your partner(s) are building.

You cannot imagine how important a simple document of this sort can be when the business hits one of the inevitable bumps along the way, and the finger-pointing starts.

When you do hit a snag in implementing your business model, it would be at this point that you and your partner(s) would sit down with your Planning Workbook and review it alongside your Duty Roster. You and your partner(s) would then rework the portion of your plans and/or assignment of duties that doesn't seem to be working.

A few tweaks of your business planning and/or a small revision of your partnership duties may be all it takes to get the business—and your "partnership"—back on track.

When Partnerships Need Financing

Partnerships often have enough startup money between the partners to get the business started. If not, the partnership will need to raise money just like any other small startup.

This will normally involve preparation of a Business Blueprint, as described prior. This Business Blueprint would be used with family and friends, as well as certain Angel Investors.

In the event you are going to need more funding than you can raise through family and friends, you will have to turn to professional outside investors.

When dealing with professional investors—whether you are a solo entrepreneur, or a partnership—you will need to create a much more formal *Business Plan for Investors*, which we'll discuss in the next chapter.

Chapter 7 —

Business Plan for Investors

This is the type of *Business Plan* that everyone thinks about when they hear, or read, something about needing a "Business Plan."

It is also something that the vast majority of new business startups will *NEVER* need to create.

Remember, less than 4,000 venture capital deals are closed each year, and only about 1,000 of those few are for early stage startups.

That then leaves over 6 million startups each year that do NOT receive venture capital.

Then, there are the *Angel Investors.* The Angel investing arena is pretty "wonky" these days with all forms of new methods of financing. But, there will still be those Angel Investors out there who will want to see your complete formal Business Plan — if for no other reason than to see if you have done your homework and know what you're talking about.

I will point out, however, that you should be aware that Angel Investors only invest in maybe 30 to 50 times as many startups as VCs do. That still leaves most of the 6+ Million new business startups this year without needing to create a "formal" Business Plan.

Having said all that, let's assume that there are a few thousand potential startups out there with high-tech ideas and high-growth potential, and you are searching for investor capital.

In which case you should have a formal, well prepared, *Business Plan*.

There is a mountain of information available about creating a formal Business Plan for investors, and all of it is very similar. So, I included in the *Appendix*, a detailed outline of the format recommended by the *Small Business Administration* (SBA).

It is a standard format that can be used by all industries, so you may have to tweak it a bit to fit your specific business.

More important, I want to provide you with some practical suggestions, and information, on preparing and presenting your *Business Plan for investors.*

Having worked on both sides of this subject, I may have a little different slant on how to approach investors, so let's take a look at some tips on developing and using your formal Business Plan.

Tips for Creating a Business Plan for Investors

Regardless of whether you are creating a formal Business Plan for an Angel Investor or a Venture Capitalist, there are certain things you need to pay very close attention to when preparing your plan:

Prepare Your "Presentation Script" First

At some point you will need to give a presentation in person to investors and you will need a script to guide you in preparing your presentation.

Your script for your personal presentation can then be the best form of an outline for creating a written Business Plan. As you visualize giving your presentation ("pitch"), it allows you to be more "in-the-moment" while you are writing your plan.

There is an entire chapter later in this book on the subject of "pitches," and how to create them — including the script.

Keep Your Business Plan Up To Date

Business plans have a very short shelf life and you never know when you might get that call to make your pitch, or deliver your written plan. So, don't let your business plan get stale … keep it "investor ready."

Use a Proper Writing Style

Use short, simple sentences — no run-on compound sentences.

Don't make broad sweeping statements about your business, your competition, or your markets. Eliminate all adjectives that have no substance but that sound impressive (to you), like "conservative," "next generation," "dynamic," and the like.

Make Your Plan Tell a Story

Tell your audience who is going to benefit from your new business idea, and how. Make it interesting — but believable — reading. The story must be true and accurate.

Don't Leave Information Gaps

If you are seeking investor money, but fail to include an exit strategy, your plan will never fly. Just don't talk about how much money everyone will make if they invest in your business ... investors will figure that out for themselves.

When you talk about your management team, make sure all resumes are complete and there are no gaps.

In your marketing section, be sure to profile your typical customer, or segment of the market. Double-check everything after creating a business plan, to make sure you have no gaps in your information.

Make it Read Smoothly

It doesn't look good if you only provide details in certain areas and not others. If you go into great detail about marketing, but gloss over technology, it makes it look like you are weak on technology. Make your level of detail consistent and read smoothly.

Never Use Negative Terms

Your Business Plan is all about what your business can do, not what your competition *can't* do. Explicit comparisons are fine, but successful entrepreneurs don't become successful by bad-mouthing their competitors.

Stay Away From Fancy Titles

You're a startup company, and it aggravates investors when all three or four founders have "C" level titles. Give the head person a title so everyone will know whom the leader is, and then hold off on fancy titles — they're annoying.

Wages and Salaries

Investors deal with startups every day, so they know how much the founders sacrifice, but sacrifice needs to end when you are creating a Business Plan for investors. Provide for reasonable (emphasis on "reasonable") wages and salaries for everyone in your organization — investors will expect that and respect you for including it.

Eliminate Non-essentials

No investor is going to be happy giving you money to buy better stuff around your office than they have in theirs, so keep the projected expense for "stuff" very conservative. Keep it simple, keep it Spartan, and eliminate the swag.

Price vs. Quality

Unless you are in the commodities business, don't try to be the low priced business in your industry. Investors know that you don't increase market share by lowering your prices — you do it through differentiation and segmentation. Investors will be looking for this in your business plan ... so be warned.

Pie-in-the-sky Profits

This has probably killed more funding deals than anything else. Investors want to work with entrepreneurs who have a true sense of the real world they will be starting their business in.

Extraordinary sales, and higher than normal industry profit ratios tell the investor that you really don't know your industry — and are someone they do NOT want to do business with.

Don't Write a Book

The more pages in your business plan — the less likely it will be read. A good target size is between 15 and 20 pages, depending on your business, but never more than 25 pages regardless.

You also should minimize the information you put into the Appendix ... use summary formats and leave all the details and fine print for later.

Read, Edit, Read, Edit, ...

The current age of "cybertext" language won't cut it in your Business Plan. Professional investors expect you to be able to write properly in your country's native language.

Make sure there are no typos, or misspelled words, and that all sentences are complete and properly formatted. Watch out for correct punctuation, and then have a professional copyeditor edit your Business Plan.

Write a "Killer" Executive Summary

This subject is covered in more detail in the next chapter, because it is one of the most important parts of your Business Plan.

Following are some additional tips, on "presenting" your Business Plan to investors:

Approach The Right Investor

You don't want to send your Business Plan or Executive Summary to the wrong type of investor. Find out early on, what an investor's specialty is. If they are heavy into construction, and your new business is high-tech ... move on to another investor.

Otherwise, you are just making a bad name for yourself in the investment community. This is a pet peeve of most of the professional investors.

Send Your Plan to a Specific Person

Here is a perfect reason for a personal introduction and referral. Rarely, if ever, does an investor fund a business plan that comes in "over the transom."

With an introduction, you can call your new contact and ask them to whom you should direct your material.

With a specific name, and a cover letter mentioning who suggested that you send your Business Plan (or Executive Summary) to them, you stand a very good chance of your document being thoroughly read.

Also, while creating a Business Plan, try to visualize writing to a single businessperson. Then your plan won't read like you're giving a speech.

Find Opportunities to Present Your Business Plan

There are many investor "events" held around the nation where you can submit your business plan for review, and if the organizers like your plan, they will invite you to make a full personal presentation.

This is a tremendous opportunity for those of you who are unable to obtain that personal introduction, or a referral.

Moreover, many of these events offer training workshops on creating a Business Plan and pitch, and how best to present them. They usually charge a modest fee for these workshops.

Forget Non-disclosure Agreements

Do not ask an A-tier Venture Capitalist, and also certain Angel Investors, to sign a non-disclosure agreement in order to see your Business Plan. They are far too busy to bother with them, but more important, if there were no initial trust the deal probably wouldn't work anyway.

There is a time and place for using a non-disclosure, but never tell a VC you will show them your business plan if they sign a non-disclosure. Most A-tier VCs won't—and they certainly have enough business plans to review without looking at yours.

Don't "Shotgun" Your Business Plan

One of the early questions you may be asked by an investor, is "… who else has seen your business plan?" If you tell them you sent out 100 copies to all the Venture Capitalists you could find listed—and not yet been funded—you just sealed your fate to rejection by this investor as well. If none of those investors were interested, why should this one be interested?

Be very judicious in who you pitch to … that's another reason why personal introductions and referrals are so important.

There you have it — some tips and added information on creating a successful *Business Plan for Investors* ... and how best to present it.

I mentioned earlier that your Executive Summary is an extremely important document when searching for professional investor financing. I believe it is so important that I have devoted the entire next chapter to discussion on the *Executive Summary*.

Chapter 8 —

Executive Summary

I am using the term "Executive Summary" here, because it is the standard term in the investment community for a short document describing all aspects of your business.

Contrary to popular belief, it is *NOT* a condensed version of your Business Plan. An Executive Summary is a concise presentation of your *business*. Its primary purpose is to "sell" your business idea to an investor so they will want to see more details about your business — either your formal Business Plan, your Pitch, or both.

It is called a business plan Executive Summary because it is also included as the introduction section of your formal Business Plan for investors. It is always the first section of your plan.

An Executive Summary is not required in the *Business Blueprint* document, because the two documents are very similar in format and content.

If you are seeking money from large professional investment sources, quite often an Executive Summary is either the first, or only, document an investor will look at before they decide whether to consider your entire Business Plan or listen to your Pitch.

Your Executive Summary must convince investors to ask you for a complete "pitch," or a copy of your complete formal Business Plan. That is why this document is so important, and why it must be carefully crafted. It is the key for entering the world of the outside professional investor.

Getting Started

So, how do you go about writing a business plan Executive Summary? There are many who believe that you need to write your complete formal Business Plan first, and then use that information to prepare your executive summary.

The second group believes your Executive Summary should be created first, and your Business Plan simply expands on the content of your Executive Summary.

Since, at some stage of your search for substantial venture capital money, you will need to prepare a "presentation," or "pitch," for investors, I recommend you first create a transcript for your pitch, and visualize yourself presenting it in front of investors.

Then, use your transcript as an outline and writing guide for your Executive Summary.

However you decide to approach writing your Executive Summary, there are several key components that must be included:

The Hook

Like any good sales copy, you need to get the attention of your reader immediately — you have precious little time to convince the reader to continue reading. Anything of a dramatic (and appropriate) nature should be presented as early as possible ... an invention ... a medical breakthrough ... a high-profile person on your management team ... anything that is special or noteworthy about your new business concept.

In one statement you need to present the unique solution you have come up with to solve a huge, and real, problem. Always lead with your "best" material.

Your Product

This is where you describe a major problem in your industry that you have a solution for. Be specific. Keep it simple. No acronyms. You also need to describe where your company will fit into the current scheme of things, and how your involvement will affect the industry by solving this major problem. How your product(s) can benefit your industry.

The Market

You will need to describe the potential market your business is addressing. How big it is ... how mature it is ... how well defined it is ... how fast it is growing ... how easy (or difficult) it is to enter ... and the portion of the market you intend to capture (be careful here — no pie-in-the-sky numbers).

If you are already receiving sales, or have done test marketing, say so here.

Your Business

This is where you tell your reader why and how you are going to beat out the competition (and you do have competition even if it is only the status quo). Be clear here in describing your competition and exactly what your advantages are over them.

You will need to convince an investor that your potential market will actually "pay" for what you have to offer. You should also be able to offer a five-year projection of how much, or how many, of what you are offering you anticipate selling.

Your Team

To many investors this is the most important part of your business plan Executive Summary. An investor is keenly interested in who will be accomplishing all your claims of success. If you have special talents on your team, say so, but don't blow anyone's accomplishments out of proportion.

Financial Projections Summary

Investors expect to receive a lot of money in return for investing in your business, and this is where you show that. Provide five years projected revenues and expenses, and be sure your numbers pass the reasonableness test.

Investors know what margins can be attained in every category of business and if you are not within the norm, you may be dismissed as not being experienced enough to run a company.

The Request

Investors will expect you to be very specific about asking for their money, as well as what you are willing to give up to get it. You also need to tell them if you will need additional rounds of funding—and when.

Don't scrimp here, because your investors will not be happy if you run out of money before you said you would.

O.K., that is about it for your business plan Executive Summary. Simple: right? **Wrong!** Writing this document is no easy task, because much information needs to be presented in a very short document—some say a maximum of *one* page. I usually suggest two, but never more than three, pages.

If you can "hook" your reader in the first paragraph, they will appreciate having enough information to determine whether they want a "pitch" or not. If you lose your reader in the first paragraph ... it won't matter how long or short your document is—you'll never get them back.

Using Your Executive Summary

What do you do with your business plan Executive Summary once it is completed? First of all, it is the first section of your formal Business Plan—which obviously, you want to complete before you start circulating your executive summary.

You never want to tell a prospective investor who likes your Executive Summary that you can't show them your Business Plan because it is not completed.

Most important, this is your "sales" document ... your brochure if you will, and you want to make sure that every contact you make has a copy. You should meet with your attorney and accountant, and make sure they have a few copies to pass to their clients who make investments.

You do the same with your banker, and every member of your Advisory Board. All these people should be arranging introductions for you with people you would also leave a copy with.

When networking, both formally and informally, you should leave copies with anyone you believe could introduce you to a prospective investor. Never leave home without a couple of copies of your Executive Summary in your pocket.

You can be judicious about who you give copies to, but if you're paranoid about someone stealing your idea, or knowing "too much" about the details of your business ... you stand a good chance of never getting your business funded.

Assuming your Executive Summary and Business Plan were successful in getting you the opportunity for a face-to-face meeting with an investor, your next objective is to polish your "pitch."

We'll discuss the *Pitch* in the next chapter.

Chapter 9 —

The Pitch

Both before and after you start your business there will be a whole host of people who will want to know about your business.

This could include investors (if you have, or need, any), advisors, bankers, suppliers, some job applicants, etc.

As a result, you will need to have a number of different descriptions — or "pitches" — for your business, ready to present in response to a wide variety of requests and questions.

Every pitch you give must have the same elements as any Business Blueprint, Plan, or Executive Summary you may develop.

Since you have already created either your Business Blueprint, or your Executive Summary/Business Plan from the transcript of your pitch, you already know what your pitch is. Now, you just need to tweak each presentation a little bit depending on your audience.

For instance: The pitch you give to your Uncle Al may be slightly different from the pitch you give to your Father; or the one you might give to your college roommate.

Here is a list of the types of pitches you may be expected to give, along with an explanation of how they should be prepared and delivered:

The 10-second Pitch

Can you describe your business in 10 seconds or less, and include all the elements described in previous chapters? If you can't … you don't have a complete understanding of your business — and your audience will know it.

This is an extremely important pitch, because you never know where your money might come from. You may be at a family reunion and rekindle acquaintances with a long lost cousin who asks what you do.

This cousin might be an accredited investor who likes to invest in early stage startups — especially for family members. Your pitch had better be good.

Or, you might be at a convention, seminar, conference, or the like, and during a coffee break and mingling, someone asks what you do. You had better be prepared to give your entire story within 10 seconds or less. That might be an interested investor you're talking to.

The examples could go on forever, but I think you get the picture.

Consider the concept of fishing, and your 10-second pitch is your bait. If your listener displays a real interest, you have them hooked for the next pitch, which is a 30-second extension of your 10-second one.

The 30-second Pitch

When your listener expresses an interest, this is where you get to emphasize the special attractions of your business. They may be technical, innovative, market, product, or whatever, but the uniqueness of your new business should be the feature of this pitch.

This is not where you emphasize the financial performance of your business — that is often what turns listeners off at this early stage of your pitches.

The objective of this pitch is to get your listener to ask for more information. That is when you need to have your 2-minute pitch ready to go.

The 2-minute Pitch

If you have ever watched *Shark Tank*, you have seen people who are looking for money from the Sharks give a short pitch after they first walk into the room.

This is a perfect example of how *NOT* to give your pitch. I haven't seen all the episodes, but neither have I ever seen one applicant give a pitch that told a complete story about their business and their needs in that couple of minutes allotted. Usually, the sharks have to drag important information out of the presenters.

It is important to let the audience know that you know your business inside and out and are capable of leading your business — all within 2 minutes, or less.

If your listener is still interested after you complete your pitch, it would be appropriate to offer that listener a copy of your Business Blueprint or your Executive Summary, depending on who you were pitching to.

Remember, you never know when, or in what setting you might be required to give a pitch, so it is very important that you have these pitches committed to memory.

The Investor Pitch

This pitch is totally different from the ones described above, in that it is usually given at an investor's request, and you will have time to properly prepare in advance.

Unlike the *Shark Tank*, which operates on "Hollywood" time, a real investor pitch will usually be 10+ minutes, with a following question and answer period.

An investor pitch is also usually accompanied by presentation aids like a *PowerPoint* presentation, or a company video, etc.

If your business requires a substantial investment from professional investors (Angel or Venture Capitalist), it is keenly important that this pitch be the very best it can be.

I suggest rehearsing the script in front of a critical audience over and over until the entire presentation becomes second nature.

Professional investors don't have time to listen to someone stumble around trying to explain what they think their business might become, and what they might need. Leave that to the *Shark Tank* folks.

Well, I realize we spent a great deal of time on pitching your business to investors, and most of you will never have to do that. But many other new entrepreneurs will need to acquire financing from someone, somewhere — probably their "Uncle Al."

If your requirements are modest, and you're going to seek funding from friends and family, the shorter, less technical pitches and Business Blueprint are adequate. Fortunately, this will be the case with the majority of new business startups.

If you will need multiple rounds of funding, you will need to involve larger Angel Investors or Venture Capitalists. In these cases you will need to be more technical and thorough in your presentations and Business Plan.

Let's assume your business is up and running, and is growing rapidly — but you don't have enough cash flow to support necessary expansion. The next chapter provides a discussion on a different kind of planning — *Business Expansion Planning.*

Chapter 10 —

Business Expansion Planning

Business expansion planning falls into two major areas: (A) operational planning — which plans out the physical needs of the expansion, and (B) financial planning — how to pay for your physical expansion.

Only you, the business owner, can do the operational planning, since no one knows your business like you do.

Of course, you should add a new section to your Planning Workbook, or start an entirely new workbook just for your expansion planning.

The second area of expansion planning — "financial planning" — is a little more complicated; so let's discuss financial planning in a little more depth.

The financial side of business expansion planning can be broken down into two separate considerations:

*(1) expansions that require a **loan** to accomplish.*

*(2) expansions that require **equity capital** to accomplish.*

We'll look at these two areas of potential financing for your expansion separately.

Loans

When planning for an expansion requiring a loan to complete, it is important to understand whom you are preparing this business plan for; who your audience will be.

The people who will be looking at this plan will likely be financial types ... bankers, loan officers, etc. (although it could be your "Uncle Al" again). Their primary interest will be your ability to repay the loan.

If you are just interested in small business equipment financing, you often can simply update your Business Blueprint, or Executive Summary; add a good performance history for your business, include a strong balance sheet, and present a plausible reason for needing the equipment. This could be your *Business Expansion Plan*.

If the expansion is a little more involved than just buying some equipment, and doing minor building refurbishment, your banker may suggest looking to the Small Business Administration (SBA) for a loan guarantee. In this case, your planning becomes a little more formal.

Here are the things you will need to add to your Business Blueprint or Executive Summary to make your expansion plan better fit the situation:

— A brief, but complete description of why you are looking to borrow money.

— A summary of your past financial performance coupled with pro-forma numbers showing how your expansion will positively impact your business. (Don't get carried away here — summary information is adequate.)

— A brief description of any major event that has occurred in your business since you prepared your last Business Blueprint or Executive Summary; like a new major contract, or new major customers, or the hiring of a new talent that increased the capability of your business. Anything truly positive you can present to your banker.

— A specific request for the loan, including the amount, the interest rate, the term, and the collateral you are willing to put up. Be precise, but certainly not demanding.

— An Appendix containing recent historical financial statements showing how well your business has been doing. This is essential.

Don't make your written expansion plan fancy or pretentious — and present it in person to your banker, or someone they may have recommended.

Just remember … if your business has not been performing extremely well, or you have very little collateral to offer, and your credit is poor — you will likely not get a loan.

However, if you are unable to obtain a loan from your banker or any other lending institution, you may then need to look to equity capital to fund your business expansion.

Equity Capital

Searching for equity capital is the second consideration of financial planning for your business expansion. You will need to seek out an Angel Investor or Venture Capitalist, depending on the size of your project, as well as the size of your business. (At this point, you may be beyond seeking equity capital from family and friends, depending on your specific situation.)

If you used professional investors for your startup, you now need to update your previous Business Plan and emphasize the significance of your expansion.

If this is your first encounter with a professional investor, you will need to write a formal Business Plan. Remember that investors will want to know everything about you and your business before they even talk about investing money in your expansion.

The format for your Business Expansion Plan will be exactly like the format you used for your startup Business Blueprint, or Business Plan, except in this case you will put much more emphasis on what your business has accomplished so far, plus why it is expected to continue growing and become even more successful.

The planning document and pitch you give to a potential investor will also need to emphasize exactly how the investor will get their money back, and how much profit they will make on their investment. (You may need an updated exit strategy here.)

For further information on finding money to support your business expansion planning, I suggest you read *Bootstrapping: And Other Alternative Ways to Finance Your Small Business.* (Available at Amazon.com — and other book sellers.)

Summary

Well, there you have it. The vast majority of businesses will never need to write a complete formal Business Plan. And many of you may not need to write *any* kind of Business Plan. Just never forget that in order to be successful, you will need to maintain ongoing up-to-date "planning."

We also concentrated on the necessity to write down your plans—both for your business and your life.

One of the best ways to do this is with a *Planning Workbook*, which we discussed in some detail—although your written planning document can be in any form that suits you.

For those few who will need to share their business planning, we discussed the various types of plans that might be required, depending on the audience. The Business Blueprint for family and friends will not be the same as the plan for an A-tier Venture Capitalist.

For dealing with professional investors, we've also provided an outline for a complete formal Business Plan, as provided by the *SBA* (included in the following Appendix).

Writing a Business Blueprint or Plan is only part of the job of soliciting money from potential investors ... your plans will need to be verbally presented in person to investors. We call that the "Pitch," and we dug into that process as well.

Even if you don't need to write a Business Plan initially, you may grow to the point where you need substantial outside money to implement your expansion plans. In this case we discussed the creation of a special document — a Business Plan — that supports your request for money for your expansion.

Regardless of where you are at with your idea and your business planning — just remember that a *Business Plan* is rarely necessary — but on-going *planning* is essential.

About the Author

My name is Bob Foster and my background spans a few decades. It is also unusually eclectic in that it includes working with the smallest of small businesses as well as Fortune 100 companies.

I have worked as CEO or consultant at businesses from the high-tech world of the "Silicon Forest," to the commercial fishing grounds of Alaska and Mexico.

I've worked on projects involving products from beer to computers, and in industries from pulp and paper to urban renewal.

Along the way I earned a reputation for saving businesses that were deemed unsalvageable.

I started businesses and sold businesses, and was lied to by large multi-national corporations (according to the late *Wilson Harrell*, all big corporations lie). As an entrepreneur, I felt the excitement of success as well as the sting of failure.

Even though I spent part of my career working for large corporations, it is the small business arena that excites me — where Entrepreneurs are born and flourish.

So, that is the foundation and background upon which I am now sharing with entrepreneurs everywhere — what I learned from real experiences, not just in classrooms.

My goal is to fan the flames of the entrepreneurial spirit, and to encourage and nurture the entrepreneur in us all.

Good luck, and I wish you much success! — Bob Foster

Contact:

bob@business-solutions-and-resources.com

Website:

http://www.business-solutions-and-resources.com

APPENDIX

SBA Guideline for a Business Plan

You can search the Internet for "Business Plans" and find thousands of websites that offer everything from free templates to very expensive services that write your plan for you.

I even discuss a few of the more popular Business Plan templates on my website http://www.business-solutions-and-resources.com

However, I have included here the Small Business Administration (SBA) *guideline for a formal Business Plan for investors, because it provides all the elements a larger investor looks for.*

This is not a template, but a guide as to what your Business Plan should contain, and how the information should be organized. If you need additional information about this guideline, you can go to the SBA *planning site at* http://1.usa.gov/wOVuhw

Keep in mind that only a few thousand of the over 6 Million new business startups in the U.S. this year will ever have to write a formal plan like this.

At the same time, this guideline does bring up some excellent topics and comments you should address in your Planning Workbook for your own business.

So here is the SBA *Business Plan guideline:*

(All of the following is provided by the SBA)

SBA's Outline of a Business Plan

Executive Summary

Your executive summary is a snapshot of your business plan as a whole and touches on your company profile and goals.

If you are just starting a business, you won't have as much information as an established company. Instead, focus on your experience and background as well as the decisions that led you to start this particular enterprise.

Demonstrate that you have done thorough market analysis. Include information about a need or gap in your target market, and how your particular solutions can fill it. Convince the reader that you can succeed in your target market, then address your future plans.

Remember, your Executive Summary will be the last thing you write. *(Author's note: This statement is highly controversial – many people believe it should be the **First** thing you write.)* So the first section of the business plan that you will tackle is the Company Description section.

Company Description

Your company description provides information on what you do, what differentiates your business from others, and the markets your business serves.

This section of your business plan provides a high-level review of the different elements of your business. This is akin to an extended elevator pitch and can help readers and potential investors quickly understand the goal of your business and its unique proposition.

What to Include in Your Company Description

— *Describe the nature of your business and list the marketplace needs that you are trying to satisfy.*

— *Explain how your products and services meet these needs.*

— *List the specific consumers, organizations or businesses that your company serves or will serve.*

— *Explain the competitive advantages that you believe will make your business a success such as your location, expert personnel, efficient operations, or ability to bring value to your customers.*

Market Analysis

Before launching your business, it is essential for you to research your business industry, market and competitors.

The market analysis section of your business plan should illustrate your industry and market knowledge as well as any of your research findings and conclusions.

What to Include in Your Market Analysis

Industry Description and Outlook – Describe your industry, including its current size and historic growth rate as well as other trends and characteristics (e.g., life cycle stage, projected growth rate). Next, list the major customer groups within your industry.

Information About Your Target Market – Narrow your target market to a manageable size. Many businesses make the mistake of trying to appeal to too many target markets. Research and include the following information about your market:

Distinguishing characteristics – What are the critical needs of your potential customers? Are those needs being met? What are the demographics of the group and where are they located? Are there any seasonal or cyclical purchasing trends that may impact your business?

Size of the primary target market – In addition to the size of your market, what data can you include about the annual purchases your market makes in your industry? What is the forecasted market growth for this group?

How much market share can you gain? – What is the market share percentage and number of customers you expect to obtain in a defined geographic area? Explain the logic behind your calculation.

Pricing and gross margin targets – Define your pricing structure, gross margin levels, and any discount that you plan to use.

When you include information about any of the market tests or research studies you have completed, be sure to focus only on the results of these tests. Any other details should be included in the appendix.

Competitive Analysis – Your competitive analysis should identify your competition by product line or service and market segment. Assess the following characteristics of the competitive landscape:

- *Market share*

- *Strengths and weaknesses*

- *How important is your target market to your competitors?*

- *Are there any barriers that may hinder you as you enter the market?*

- *What is your window of opportunity to enter the market?*

— Are there any indirect or secondary competitors who may impact your success?

— What barriers to market are there (e.g., changing technology, high investment cost, lack of quality personnel)?

Regulatory Restrictions – Include any customer or governmental regulatory requirements affecting your business, and how you'll comply. Also, cite any operational or cost impact the compliance process will have on your business.

Organization and Management

Every business is structured differently. Find out the best organization and management structure for your business.

Organization and Management follows the Market Analysis. This section should include: your company's organizational structure, details about the ownership of your company, profiles of your management team, and the qualifications of your board of directors.

Who does what in your business? What is their background and why are you bringing them into the business as board members or employees? What are they responsible for? These may seem like unnecessary questions to answer in a one- or two-person organization, but the people reading your business plan want to know who's in charge, so tell them. Give a detailed description of each division or department and its function.

This section should include who's on the board (if you have an advisory board) and how you intend to keep them there. What kind of salary and benefits package do you have for your people? What incentives are you offering? How about promotions? Reassure your reader that the people you have on staff are more than just names on a letterhead.

Organizational Structure

A simple but effective way to lay out the structure of your company is to create an organizational chart with a narrative description. This will prove that you're leaving nothing to chance, you've thought out exactly who is doing what, and there is someone in charge of every function of your company. Nothing will fall through the cracks, and nothing will be done three or four times over. To a potential investor or employee, that is very important.

Ownership Information

This section should also include the legal structure of your business along with the subsequent ownership information it relates to. Have you incorporated your business? If so, is it a C or S corporation? Or perhaps you have formed a partnership with someone. If so, is it a general or limited partnership? Or maybe you are a sole proprietor.

The following important ownership information should be incorporated into your business plan:

– *Names of owners*

– *Percentage ownership*

– *Extent of involvement with the company*

– *Forms of ownership (i.e., common stock, preferred stock, general partner, limited partner)*

– *Outstanding equity equivalents (i.e., options, warrants, convertible debt)*

– *Common stock (i.e., authorized or issued)*

– *Management Profiles*

Experts agree that one of the strongest factors for success in any growth company is the ability and track record of its owner/management team, so let your reader know about the key people in your company and their backgrounds. Provide resumes that include the following information:

– *Name*

– *Position (include brief position description along with primary duties)*

– *Primary responsibilities and authority*

– *Education*

– *Unique experience and skills*

— *Prior employment*

— *Special skills*

— *Past track record*

— *Industry recognition*

— *Community involvement*

— *Number of years with company*

— *Compensation basis and levels (make sure these are reasonable -- not too high or too low)*

Be sure you quantify achievements (e.g. "Managed a sales force of ten people," "Managed a department of fifteen people," "Increased revenue by 15 percent in the first six months," "Expanded the retail outlets at the rate of two each year," "Improved the customer service as rated by our customers from a 60 percent to a 90 percent rating").

Also highlight how the people surrounding you complement your own skills. If you're just starting out, show how each person's unique experience will contribute to the success of your venture.

Board of Directors' Qualifications

The major benefit of an unpaid advisory board is that it can provide expertise that your company cannot otherwise afford. A list of well-known, successful business owners/managers can go a long way toward enhancing your company's credibility and perception of management expertise.

(Author's note: Be aware that there is a major difference between an "Advisory Board" and a "Board of Directors.")

If you have a board of directors, be sure to gather the following information when developing the outline for your business plan:

— *Names*

— *Positions on the board*

— *Extent of involvement with company*

— *Background*

— *Historical and future contribution to the company's success*

Service or Product Line

What do you sell? How does it benefit your customers? What is the product lifecycle? Get tips on how to tell the story about your product or service.

Once you've completed the Organizational and Management section of your plan, the next part of your business plan is where you describe your service or product, emphasizing the benefits to potential and current customers.

Focus on why your particular product will fill a need for your target customers.

What to Include in Your Service or Product Line Section

A Description of Your Product / Service

Include information about the specific benefits of your product or service – from your customers' perspective. You should also talk about your product or service's ability to meet consumer needs, any advantages your product has over that of the competition, and the current development stage your product is in (e.g., idea, prototype).

Details About Your Product's Life Cycle

Be sure to include information about where your product or service is in its life cycle, as well as any factors that may influence its cycle in the future.

Intellectual Property

If you have any existing, pending, or any anticipated copyright or patent filings, list them here. Also disclose whether any key aspects of a product may be classified as trade secrets. Last, include any information pertaining to existing legal agreements, such as nondisclosure or non-compete agreements.

Research and Development (R&D) Activities

101

Outline any R&D activities that you are involved in or are planning. What results of future R&D activities do you expect? Be sure to analyze the R&D efforts of not only your own business, but also of others in your industry.

Marketing and Sales

How do you plan to market your business? What is your sales strategy? Read more about how to include this information in your plan.

Once you've completed the Service or Product Line section of your plan, the next part of your business plan should focus on your marketing and sales management strategy for your business.

Marketing is the process of creating customers, and customers are the lifeblood of your business. In this section, the first thing you want to do is define your marketing strategy. There is no single way to approach a marketing strategy; your strategy should be part of an ongoing business-evaluation process and unique to your company. However, there are common steps you can follow which will help you think through the direction and tactics you would like to use to drive sales and sustain customer loyalty.

An **overall marketing strategy** should include four different strategies:

    – A market penetration strategy.

— A growth strategy. This strategy for building your business might include: an internal strategy such as how to increase your human resources, an acquisition strategy such as buying another business, a franchise strategy for branching out, a horizontal strategy where you would provide the same type of products to different users, or a vertical strategy where you would continue providing the same products but would offer them at different levels of the distribution chain.

— Channels of distribution strategy. Choices for distribution channels could include original equipment manufacturers (OEMs), an internal sales force, distributors, or retailers.

— Communication strategy. How are you going to reach your customers? Usually a combination of the following tactics works the best: promotions, advertising, public relations, personal selling, and printed materials such as brochures, catalogs, flyers, etc.

After you have developed a comprehensive marketing strategy, you can then define your sales strategy. This covers how you plan to actually sell your product.

Your **overall sales strategy** should include two primary elements:

—A sales force strategy. If you are going to have a sales force, do you plan to use internal or independent representatives? How many salespeople will you recruit for your sales force? What type of recruitment strategies will you

use? How will you train your sales force? What about compensation for your sales force?

— Your sales activities. When you are defining your sales strategy, it is important that you break it down into activities. For instance, you need to identify your prospects. Once you have made a list of your prospects, you need to prioritize the contacts, selecting the leads with the highest potential to buy first. Next, identify the number of sales calls you will make over a certain period of time. From there, you need to determine the average number of sales calls you will need to make per sale, the average dollar size per sale, and the average dollar size per vendor.

Funding Request

If you are seeking funding for your business, find out about the necessary information you should include in your plan.

If you are seeking funding for your business venture, use this section to outline your requirements.

Your funding request should include the following information:

— Your current funding requirement

— Any future funding requirements over the next five years

— How you intend to use the funds you receive: Is the funding request for capital expenditures? Working capital? Debt

retirement? Acquisitions? Whatever it is, be sure to list it in this section.

— Any strategic financial situational plans for the future, such as: a buyout, being acquired, debt repayment plan, or selling your business. These areas are extremely important to a future creditor, since they will directly impact your ability to repay your loan(s).

When you are outlining your funding requirements, include the amount you want now and the amount you want in the future. Also include the time period that each request will cover, the type of funding you would like to have (e.g., equity, debt), and the terms that you would like to have applied.

To support your funding request you'll also need to provide historical and prospective financial information.

Financial Projections

If you need funding, providing financial projections to back up your request is critical. Find out what information you need to include in your financial projections for your small business.

Financial Projections

You should develop the Financial Projections section after you've analyzed the market and set clear objectives. That's when you can allocate resources efficiently. The following is a list of the critical financial statements to include in your business plan packet.

Historical Financial Data

If you own an established business, you will be requested to supply historical data related to your company's performance. Most creditors request data for the last three to five years, depending on the length of time you have been in business.

The historical financial data to include are your company's income statements, balance sheets, and cash flow statements for each year you have been in business (usually for up to three to five years). Often, creditors are also interested in any collateral that you may have that could be used to ensure your loan, regardless of the stage of your business.

Prospective Financial Data

All businesses, whether startup or growing, will be required to supply prospective financial data. Most of the time, creditors will want to see what you expect your company to be able to do within the next five years. Each year's documents should include forecasted income statements, balance sheets, cash flow statements, and capital expenditure budgets. For the first year, you should supply monthly or quarterly projections. After that, you can stretch it to quarterly and/or yearly projections for years two through five.

Make sure that your projections match your funding requests; creditors will be on the lookout for inconsistencies. It's much better if you catch mistakes before they do. If you have made assumptions in your projections, be sure to summarize what you have assumed. This way, the reader will not be left guessing.

Finally, include a short analysis of your financial information. Include a ratio and trend analysis for all of your financial statements (both historical and prospective). Since pictures speak louder than words, you may want to add graphs of your trend analysis (especially if they are positive).

Appendix

An appendix is optional, but a useful place to include information such as resumes, permits and leases.

The Appendix should be provided to readers on an as-needed basis. In other words, it should not be included with the main body of your business plan. Your plan is your communication tool; as such, it will be seen by a lot of people. Some of the information in the business section you will not want everyone to see, but specific individuals (such as creditors) may want access to this information to make lending decisions. Therefore, it is important to have the appendix within easy reach.

The appendix would include:

    – Credit history (personal & business)

— *Resumes of key managers*

— *Product pictures*

— *Letters of reference*

— *Details of market studies*

— *Relevant magazine articles or book references*

— *Licenses, permits or patents*

— *Legal documents*

— *Copies of leases*

— *Building permits*

— *Contracts*

— *List of business consultants, including attorney and accountant*

Any copies of your business plan should be controlled; keep a distribution record. This will allow you to update and maintain your business plan on an as-needed basis. Remember, too, that when raising capital, you should include a private placement disclaimer with your business plan.

www.ingramcontent.com/pod-product-compliance
Lightning Source LLC
Chambersburg PA
CBHW051335170526
45166CB00002B/817